D0644011

First Facts

Animal Rulers

KINGS OF THE OCEANS

by Jody S. Rake

Consultant:
Jackie Gai, DVM
Wildlife Veterinarian

CAPSTONE PRESS
a capstone imprint

First Facts are published by Capstone Press,
1710 Roe Crest Drive, North Mankato, Minnesota 56003
www.mycapstone.com

Library of Congress Cataloging-in-Publication Data
Library of Congress cataloging-in-Publication Data is available on the Library of
Congress website.

ISBN: 978-1-5157-8066-3 (library binding) — 978-1-5157-8072-4 (paperback) —
978-1-5157-8079-6 (eBook PDF)

Editorial Credits
Adrian Vigliano, editor; Kayla Rossow, designer; Kelly Garvin, media researcher;
Kathy McColley, production specialist

Photo Credits
Minden Pictures/Fred Bavendam, 21; Newscom/Gerard LACZ_VWPics, 7;
Shutterstock: Alex Zaitsev, cover (middle), Borisoff, 5, FloridaStock, 15, Gino
Santa Maria, cover (top right), 19, Jono Gaza, 11, magnusdeepbelow, 13, Mogens
Trolle, 17, nudiblue, cover (top left), Seaphotoart, cover (bottom), wildestanimal,
cover (top middle), Willyam Bradberry, 9

Artistic Elements
Shutterstock: Airin.dizain, Alemon cz, AlexZaitsev, Ann Doronina, daulon, irabel8,
LIORIKI, littlesam, Miceking, Seaphotoart, Vector Tradition SM, white whale,
Willyam Bradberry

Printed and bound in China.
004727

Table of Contents

Oceans Full of Animals

Oceans cover most of Earth's surface. They are wide and deep. Ocean water is salty and full of life. Ocean **food chains** create giant **food webs**. At the top of them are **predators**. They are the rulers of the oceans!

food chain—a series of plants and animals in which each one in the series eats the one before it

food web—many food chains connected to one another

predator—an animal that hunts other animals for food

Orca

Orcas are **apex** predators. They live in all oceans, but most live closer to the poles. Male orcas can be 19 to 22 feet (5.8 to 6.7 meters) long. But it's not just size that makes orcas amazing. Intelligence and teamwork make orcas great hunters. They feed on fish, squid, and seals. But together, a **pod** of orcas can attack a bigger whale!

apex—the top predator of a food chain
pod—a group of whales

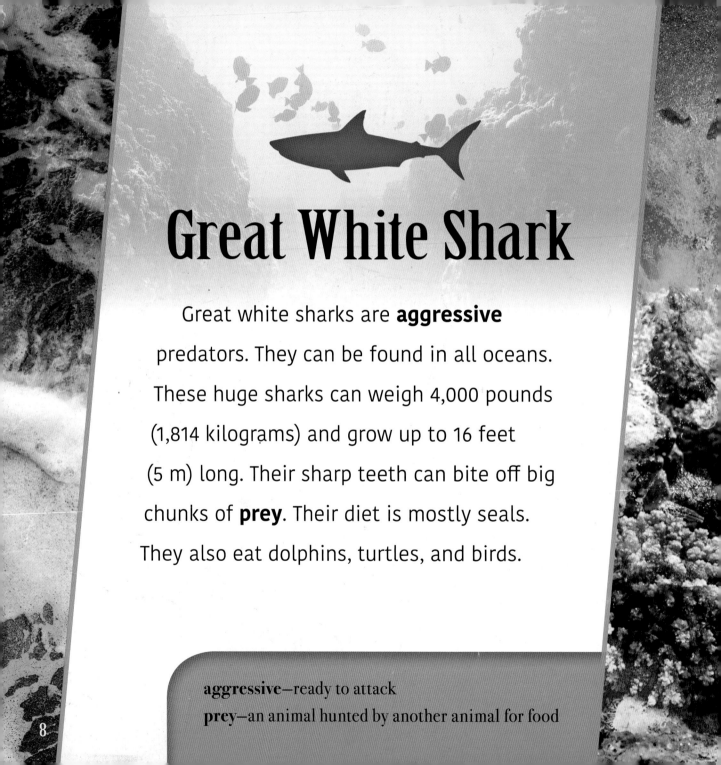

Great White Shark

Great white sharks are **aggressive** predators. They can be found in all oceans. These huge sharks can weigh 4,000 pounds (1,814 kilograms) and grow up to 16 feet (5 m) long. Their sharp teeth can bite off big chunks of **prey**. Their diet is mostly seals. They also eat dolphins, turtles, and birds.

aggressive—ready to attack
prey—an animal hunted by another animal for food

Fact! Shark attacks on humans are rare.
There are only about 35 attacks each year.

Goliath Grouper

Goliath groupers are sea giants.
They live in the Atlantic Ocean. These
fish grow up to 8 feet (2.4 m) long and
weigh 800 pounds (363 kg). Goliath
groupers eat almost any prey that will fit
in their huge mouths. Their prey includes
fish, lobsters, octopuses, and turtles.

11

Ray

About 200 ray **species** live in oceans around the world. Most search the sea floor for shellfish to eat. Some rays swim through the open sea.

The manta ray has a "wingspan" of up to 23 feet (7 m). It is wider than most whales are long! This ocean giant eats **plankton**.

species—a group of animals with similar features
plankton—tiny plants and animals that drift in the ocean

13

Polar Bear

Polar bears are top Arctic predators. They depend on the ocean for food. Much of the Arctic Ocean has a frozen surface for most of the year. Arctic seals swim under the ice. Polar bears hunt seals from above the ice. They wait for seals to come up for air. Polar bears may swim many miles in search of places to hunt.

Leopard Seal

Antarctica is full of animal life. Penguins, seabirds, and seals make this frozen world their home. The leopard seal is a fierce predator on land and in the sea. Leopard seals are named for their spotted fur. With their wide mouths and sharp teeth, they snag most Antarctic prey — even other seals.

Fact! The leopard seal is the only seal that eats other warm-blooded prey.

Box Jellyfish

All jellyfish have stinging **tentacles**.
But no jellyfish is as feared as the
box jellyfish of the Pacific Ocean.
Their 10-foot (3-m) tentacles have
lots of stingers. Each stinger contains
powerful **venom** that stuns or kills
prey. Box jellyfish use their stingers
to hunt fish and shrimp.

tentacle—a long, flexible limb used for moving,
feeling, and grabbing
venom—a poisonous liquid made by an animal
to kill its prey

Fact! The box jellyfish is one of the most dangerous animals on Earth. Its sting can make a human go into shock and drown.

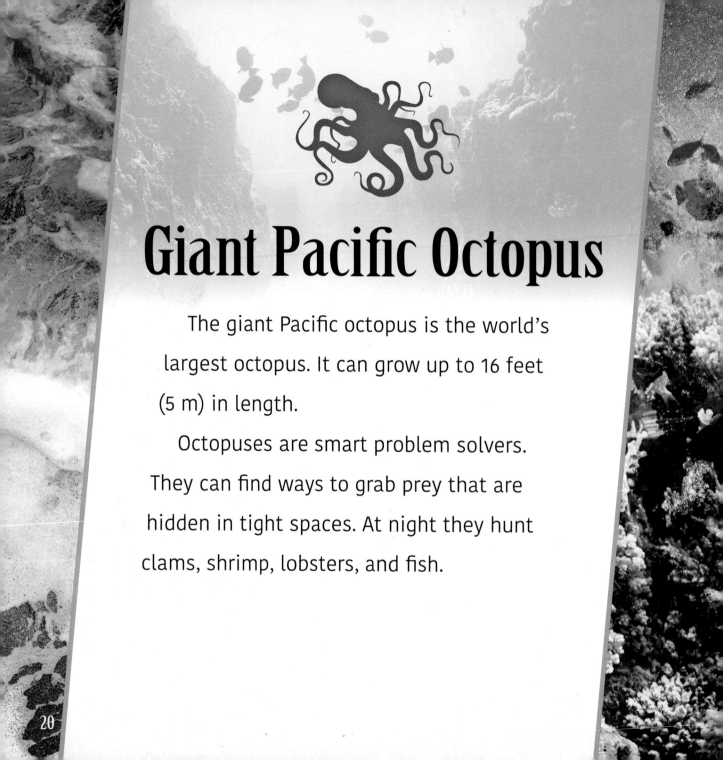

Giant Pacific Octopus

The giant Pacific octopus is the world's largest octopus. It can grow up to 16 feet (5 m) in length.

Octopuses are smart problem solvers. They can find ways to grab prey that are hidden in tight spaces. At night they hunt clams, shrimp, lobsters, and fish.

Fact! The giant Pacific octopus can change its skin color to blend into its surroundings.

Glossary

agressive (uh-GREH-siv)—ready to attack

apex (AY-pecks)—the top predator of a food chain

food chain (FOOD CHAYN)—a series of plants and animals in which each one in the series eats the one before it

food web (FOOD WEB)—many food chains connected to one another

plankton (PLANGK-tuhn)—tiny plants and animals that drift in the ocean

pod (POD)—a group of whales

predator (PRED-uh-tur)—an animal that hunts other animals for food

prey (PRAY)—an animal hunted by another animal for food

species (SPEE-sheez)—a group of animals with similar features

tentacle (TEN-tuh-kuhl)—a long, flexible limb used for moving, feeling, and grabbing

venom (VEN-uhm)—a poisonous liquid made by an animal to kill its prey

Read More

Gerber, Carole. *Stingrays!: Underwater Fliers*. Step Into Reading. New York: Random House, 2015.

Gregory, Josh. *Great White Sharks*. Nature's Children. New York: Children's Press, 2014.

Zuchora-Walske, Christine. *Killer Whales: Built for the Hunt*. Predator Profiles. North Mankato, Minn.: Capstone Press, 2016.

Internet Sites

Use Facthound to find Internet sites related to this book.

Visit *www.facthound.com*

Just type in 9781515780663 and go!

Check out projects, games and lots more at
www.capstonekids.com

Critical Thinking Questions

1. List two things about oceans. How are oceans different from land?

2. Study the picture of the grouper on page 11. Then study the picture of the ray on page 13. What similarities do these animals have? How are they different?

3. What would happen if any one of these large predators were to die out? How would their disappearance affect the habitat?

4. The box jellyfish is the most venomous marine animal in the world. What is venom? (Hint: Use your glossary for help!)

Index